YOUR HOROSCOPE 2018

TAURUS

ZOE BUCKDEN

Bring freedom to
make ∆

Uranus = Planet of ∆ =

April   Aries = Spear 12th   Uranus
3/19   House = House of Secrets
         6/18 = inner needs
         + unconscious
         Revelation

Uranus
forward
in spring

House #1 = Self

House #4
Home +
Family

10th House
Career
&
Uranus Rules!

Uranus
Retrograde
Bk to Aries

General Trends

For the past few years, you may have felt as if the world is against you. Fear not! It isn't, not at all.

What is happening is that your own unconscious mind is generating situations that you must deal with. These can be very difficult. You may confront hostility, upsets, and obstacles of all kinds. They represent hidden forces within your own mind: memories, doubts, fears, and inner conflicts.

It is best to acknowledge such things honestly. The more aware you are of these inner drives, the less control they have over you. Simply by becoming conscious of them, you gain the power to choose freely how to live your life.

The reason why your unconscious issues have flared up in this way is that Uranus is moving through Aries, your solar twelfth house of inner needs and the unconscious. Uranus is the planet of change, and its purpose is to breathe energy into our lives. Sometimes this means shattering our routines and demolishing the careful structures we have built around ourselves. Stability is a good thing, but rigidity can become a prison. No one want to be stuck in the same rut forever. Uranus brings freedom and the chance for a fresh start.

The process can be tough. You may well feel a little bruised by now. Happily, your ordeal is almost over. Uranus leaves your twelfth house in mid-May this year, to enter your own sun sign and solar first house of self. This will give you a tremendous boost in making necessary changes to all areas of your life during the next seven years.

Don't rush into any major changes of direction right away. The twelfth house is known as the house of secrets, so a lot of things may come to light as Uranus changes sign. Expect all sorts of revelations, including some ugly truths about people you thought you could trust. Accept them as calmly as you can. It is better to know than to be deceived.

Uranus will retrograde back into Aries in November, and stay for a few months before moving forward into Taurus in spring 2019. You have plenty of time to consider your options. Don't make any final decisions until well into next year.

Since Uranus rules your solar tenth house of career, you may experience its effects in your professional life. Perhaps you feel stuck, or you suddenly realise you are in completely the wrong line of work. This is good to know, but hold off on taking any action. You are due for a lot of upheaval in your career house this year, so wait and see what happens before deciding what to do.

First, we have the Leo-Aquarius series of eclipses, which began last year and continues throughout 2018. This affects your solar fourth house of home and family as well as your tenth house of career, and may change the balance between these areas of your life.

Each eclipse series is united by a common theme. By now you may have guessed what overall change this series is bringing to your life.

The process will end early next year, with a final eclipse in Leo, your solar house of home and family. Then you are done with upheaval in these areas. There will not be any more eclipses along this axis for the next seven years.

The main thing to remember about eclipses is that it is their job to open up new paths in our lives. That sometimes means closing off the path we're on. Once the eclipse has spoken, nothing can go back to the way it was. The world has changed. It is pointless to resist.

It is always best not to start anything under an eclipse. Just listen carefully to its message, and consider what it means.

Don't be in a hurry to take action. You can't see far enough ahead to make any plans or decisions. Circumstances could change in the blink of an eye. Let events unfold as they will.

You may receive the message of the eclipse exactly one month before or after the actual date of the eclipse itself. Watch out for significant events at these times.

Adding to your woes, Mars will be retrograde in your career house during the summer. This can mean frustration, depression, and pent-up anger. Mars is aggressive, and resents being held back.

3

Mars Rules House #12 — inner need
#1 = Self

Because Mars rules your house of inner needs and the unconscious, you will find the effect more powerful than any other sign. Take care not to let your feelings run away with you. As you may already know, Taurus people are seldom roused, but when it happens your rage can be explosive. This is hardly surprising, since your inner world is ruled by Mars. Be aware that the intensity of your feelings is not necessarily a sign that the problems you face are as big as they seem.

Strive to understand the situation, and accept that simply becoming aware of the issues is part of finding a solution.

Since two eclipses will fall at the same time, and on this same Leo-Aquarius axis, the atmosphere could get extremely fraught. Try to stay calm.

More than ever, it is crucial that you take no action unless absolutely necessary. Give yourself a chance to reflect on your goals and assess how best to reach them. Don't plan to initiate anything at all during these difficult months.

Be especially careful regarding safety at this time. Avoid conflict, and don't take unnecessary risks.

After this, your ruling planet Venus turns retrograde during autumn, in Scorpio, your solar house of relationships. At the same time, erratic Uranus retrogrades into Aries on the opposite side of the zodiac wheel.

This spells upheaval. Old problems and issues from the past are likely to flare up. Try to be patient.

4

You may feel held back by existing commitments. Arguments and frustration can take a toll on your health. If you have any chronic conditions, they may get worse. Do your best to manage the stress. Protect your health, and take some time out for yourself if you need it.

Because Venus is your personal ruler, you will feel this retrograde more strongly than almost any other sign. Progress will be extremely slow.

Don't fight this. You can't win. Use the time to deal with long-standing issues once and for all. You will feel so much better in a few months. 2018-2019

This will be a year of change for you. Many things come to an end, but new things are also beginning. It is best to roll with the punches and trust that you will find your feet again. Remember that it is natural for things to end. Old and outworn parts of our lives must be cleared away, so that fresh and exciting ones can flourish.

A new eclipse series on the Cancer-Capricorn axis starts in the summer of this year. The first eclipse is in Cancer, your house of day-to-day matters, and will shake up your ordinary environment. Other eclipses will follow in 2019, affecting both this house and your house of travel and learning. A new direction in life, fresh starts, and broader horizons are all on the cards. You may retrain, relocate, or find some other way to explore the fantastic opportunities this world has to offer.

The process will take two years, ending in 2020, so don't make any firm plans just yet. Just be open to new possibilities, and see what appears in your path.

Saturn is currently moving through your travel house, so don't expect things to go smoothly. Saturn's job is to test each area of our lives for weaknesses and flaws. You may find that all sorts of issues crop up in the areas of travel and learning. This is a good thing! You can only fix problems if you know about them. Work methodically towards your goals, and you will astonish yourself with what you can achieve.

Your birthday month this year will be electric. Uranus, planet of change and the unexpected, moves into your own sun sign and house of self. You also have a new moon in your own sign around the same time. These two events will give a massive boost to everything you want to do.

The most stable areas of your life this year will be money, shared property, friendship, romance, and children. No major changes are due, so enjoy things as they are.

January

For some months now, you may have felt that all the power in your life lay with other people. This is due to a cluster of planets in that part of your chart.

The situation will last for a few months. In April several of these planets will move into your own sun sign of Taurus, and things should start to improve. Until then, just accept the situation. There is nothing you can do to change it right now.

Still, the year does get off to a good start. On Tuesday 2, a full moon in Cancer, your house of day-to-day matters, brings something to an end. It's also a good time to finish things up.

This is a lovely full moon, with lots of positive energy around. It may be quite intense and emotional, so look after yourself and don't take things too much to heart.

The effects will be especially strong as the Moon rules Cancer. As long as you stay balanced, it's a great time to be with people you care about.

On Wednesday 17 a new moon in Capricorn, your house of travel and learning, signals a new beginning. It is a good time to start new projects.

This is a beautiful new moon, with happy support from powerful Pluto and your own ruling planet Venus. Mars provides an extra boost from Scorpio, your relationship house.

Anything you begin now will be immensely successful. Uranus in hard angle may bring unexpected snags, but you can find a way through them.

Get your projects off the ground early, because there will be a major shakeup at the end of the month. On Wednesday 31 a full Moon lunar eclipse in Leo, your house of home and family, ends a chapter in this area of your life.

This is a friendly eclipse, with your own ruler Venus supporting the Sun in Aquarius, your career house. Whatever happens will be for the best. It is not a good time to start anything, though. Just sit quietly and see what comes up.

This is the fourth eclipse in the Leo-Aquarius series, which started with a lunar eclipse in Leo in mid-February 2017. Since then you have undergone significant changes in the areas of home, family, and career.

You may also have started to notice connections and similarities between these events. If so, you are beginning to recognise the theme of this series, the deep transformation it will bring to your life. This year will be the crunch point, when all the necessary changes you must undergo will burst upon you. It may be unsettling, but remember it's the only way to shake you out of your routine and set you on the right path for the future.

The series will end with a lunar eclipse in Leo, your house of home and family, in January 2019. This completes the transformation of the areas of home and career. No further eclipses are due on this axis until 2026.

Listen carefully to the message of this year's eclipses, and you will benefit for years to come.

February

The main event this month is the new moon solar eclipse in Aquarius, your career house. This happens on Thursday 15, and will open a new chapter in this area of your life.

This is the fifth eclipse in the Leo-Aquarius series, and by now you may be getting a sense of the direction in which the universe is taking you. The transformation that began in early 2017 is well underway. We have one more year of change ahead of us, but then it is done.

The current eclipse may bring unexpected news and greater clarity on an issue that is important to you. Mercury in close support, and Uranus in helpful angle in Aries, will bring insight and understanding. Complex emotional matters may come to the surface. Reflect on them quietly, but do not take action unless necessary.

As always under an eclipse, it is best not to initiate anything. New moons are usually a good time for fresh starts, but with conditions changing so rapidly, there simply isn't enough information to act on. Let events unfold as they will.

After this month's eclipse, only one more takes place in Aquarius. That will be a full moon lunar eclipse in July. Since full moons bring endings, whatever begins now may well come to a conclusion at that time. Things will then stay settled in your career until the next Leo-Aquarius series begins in 2026.

The remaining two eclipses in the current series are both in Leo, one in August this year and one in January 2019. These will settle matters in the area of home and family as well, so watch out for significant events at that time.

During the second half of this month, from Monday 19 onwards, a happy cluster of planets in Pisces will light up your house of friendship. Neptune, the ruler of Pisces, enjoys the company of the Sun, Venus, and Mercury all gathered together. This is a lovely time to enjoy life's blessings in this area.

There is no full moon this month, as it occurs in early March. You may feel the effects in the last few days of this month, though. It is a friendly full moon, but may be a little subdued.

The Sun and Neptune close together in Pisces, sign of dreams and wishes, oppose the Moon in Virgo, your house of romance and children, with realistic Saturn strong in Capricorn making helpful angles to both.

This is not a time when all your wishes come true. Rather, you may have to face the reality that things didn't quite work out the way you'd hoped.

Full moons bring endings, and you may see the results of something that started under a new moon back in September last year. If they aren't quite the stuff that dreams are made of, don't be disheartened. The wonderful cluster of planets in

Pisces still weave their magic spells around all your hopes and wishes.

Also, Saturn makes lovely angles to both Sun and Moon. Remember that Saturn's job is to identify flaws and weaknesses so that we can fix them. Whatever comes up at this time, especially in the areas of romance, children, or friendship, use it to improve your plans for the future. You may get good advice from someone whose experience and knowledge you respect.

March

The month starts with a full moon in Virgo, your house of romance and children, on Friday 2. This is a time for finishing things and bringing projects to a conclusion. Anything that needs fixing, checking, or a few final touches is the perfect focus for your attention right now. Saturn helps you spot any problems, and the Sun provides you with plenty of energy to sort them out.

If things haven't quite worked out the way you expected, try not to feel disillusioned. Use this time to find out what went wrong, so you can improve for the future.

Make your plans as solid as you can. In early September, six months from now, a new moon in Virgo will provide the perfect opportunity to try again.

From Thursday 8, Jupiter will be retrograde in Scorpio, your house of relationships. Usually we don't feel the outer planets very strongly, but you may find that things slow down in this area during the next few months. Jupiter will go direct again in mid-July, leaving you plenty of time to use its protective energy before the planet moves into Sagittarius in November this year.

Also at this time you may begin to feel the effects of Mercury's turn retrograde, which happens later in the month. Mercury is the planet of speech and thought, travel and learning, buying and selling. These things don't go smoothly when the planet is retrograde, so be patient with any snags.

As Mercury is currently in Aries, your house of inner needs and the unconscious, you will feel the effects on a deeply personal level. Issues from the past may crop up and need to be dealt with. Be patient as you do this. You may need time for reflection. If so, try again in late April or early May, when the planet has gone direct.

Mercury rules your money house, so cash flow problems are possible. It's best to avoid making any big decisions or expensive purchases at this time. Don't sign any contracts if you can help it.

Take special care when travelling, and keep a close eye on your belongings. Electrical and electronic equipment may suffer glitches or breakdowns, so be prepared for repair bills and replacements.

Mercury also rules your house of romance and children, so expect some misunderstandings with your loved ones. Be patient with them, and with yourself.

If you find yourself locked in an argument, stop and take a deep breath. Your own unconscious issues could be the root of the problem.

Make an honest effort to express yourself constructively, and listen to the other person's point of view. This could lead to a deeper connection with those you love.

Mercury turns direct again in mid-April, but the effects of the retrograde will last until early May. Use this time to review past experiences, rather than start anything new. It is a time for thinking and planning, not for action.

On Saturday 17 a new moon in Pisces, your house of friendship, signals the beginning of something new. Usually it would be a good time to start projects, but with Mercury slowing down it may be wiser to wait. That said, if you have old plans that were previously shelved, or if opportunities arise from your past, this would be an ideal time to develop them further.

Don't sign contracts or make any firm commitments just yet. Leave such things until the first week in May.

On Thursday 22, Mercury turns retrograde in Aries, your house of inner needs and the unconscious. There is always a certain amount of static in the air when a planet changes direction, and Mercury is more noticeable than most. Expect all sorts of issues to crop up at this time.

Pluto in hard angle in Capricorn, your house of travel and learning, could make things worse. You may have trouble with a domineering person, or run foul of some unreasonable rule.

Your ruler Venus nearby might help, although this harmonious planet is not at its best in aggressive Aries. Conflict is likely, especially with women. Keep a low profile if you can. If you need to make a stand, state your case clearly.

On Saturday 31 a full moon in Libra, your house of health, brings something to an end. This is an extremely tense full moon, with hard angles to Saturn and Mars close together in Capricorn, your house of travel and learning. Major conflicts and angry outbursts are likely.

Tread softly. If you must hold your ground over an important matter, do it as calmly as you can.

You may experience feelings of deep frustration, anger and depression. Ill health and accidents are also possible. Take very good care of yourself.

Usually a full moon is a good time to finish things, but with all this angry tension around, you would do better to wait a few days.

Also, your ruler Venus moves into Taurus on the same date, Saturday 31. This is the first planet (except the Moon) to leave the Scorpio-Aries cluster, and there will be plenty of positive energy to follow. You will feel the effects most strongly of all the signs, since Venus is your own personal ruler. Within days you will find that the tide is turning, and things are finally going your way.

If you have projects to finish up around the time of the full moon, wait until April 3 if you can. The worst of the tension will have disappeared by then, and there will be a lovely Venus boost to help you.

April *2018*

The headline event this month is that powerful Pluto and erratic Uranus finally move out of hard angle with each other. They have been at odds since 2011, bringing major changes to everyone's lives. *Challenges in pers. growth*

If you have found the past few years difficult, especially in the areas of travel, learning, and personal growth, remember that these planets operate on a massive scale, affecting all of society. You are not alone!

The plus side of such large-scale transformation is that it frees us to let go of the past and move forward into a splendid new future. The danger is that we may throw out what is good and valuable, not just that which is outworn and no longer needed.

Be careful not to get carried away this month. A final burst of power is due, before these planets go their separate ways. It is all too easy to fling aside parts of our life, only to regret it later. Think long and hard before deciding that something needs to go. *Family → [4] Easter*

On Monday 16 a new moon in Aries, your house of inner needs and the unconscious, will bring this issue into sharp focus. Uranus close by fills the air with electrical energy, while Pluto in hard angle summons the storm. This could be an explosive time, so tread with care.

Let go of Past - move to future

Usually a new moon is a good time to begin things, but this one is so tense and frazzled that you would be wiser to wait. If you do feel the need to act, make sure you are implementing solid plans that you have already made. Don't make hasty decisions or rush into things.

Mars in Capricorn, close to sullen Pluto, is in beautiful angle to harmony planet Venus in your own sign of Taurus, and also to dreamy Neptune in Pisces and protective Jupiter retrograde in Scorpio. None of these happy planets are directly involved with the new moon, but they do suggest you could find success. There is plenty of positive energy around, if you move slowly and with caution.

The happy relations between these planets also suggest that even if disaster does strike at this fretful new moon, wonderful things are coming your way. Stay positive!

A few days later the Sun moves into your own sun sign of Taurus, and your birthday month begins. Uranus close by in your house of the unconscious helps you act in ways that reflect your true self.

This is a splendid time to reach clarity on what you want, and to begin any deep changes you feel are needed in your life. Your ruler Venus is still in your own sign, bringing harmonious energy to everything you do.

Take your first steps early, before Venus moves into Gemini on Tuesday 24. After this date, you will feel the

20

energy of your ruling planet in your money house. Use it to improve your finances. 4/30/18

On Monday 30 a full moon in Scorpio, your relationship house, brings something to an end. This is a fairly friendly moon, with idealistic Neptune and realistic Saturn both in helpful angle. You may begin to see more clearly how to reach your common goals. There may be some emotional upheaval, though, with Uranus in opposition close to the Sun. Try not to get drawn into arguments.

If you feel the need for some alone time, take it. A bit of space for quiet reflection will do you good.

Also on this date, Monday 30, Uranus and Pluto finally move away from their difficult angle to each other. You may not notice this right now, but you certainly will in the months that follow. It will be as if a cloud has lifted from your life.

Everyone is affected by this change, so expect a sense of new freedom to spread throughout the world. You may find your spirits lift, as your house of inner needs and the unconscious is involved. Obstacles to personal growth may disappear, leaving you free to pursue your dreams.

Tensions may return in the first few months of next year, but you are familiar with them now and will know how to deal with anything that crops up. From April 2019 onwards, everything will feel better and brighter.

May 2018

This month, a genuinely rare event occurs. Uranus, one of the most slow-moving planets, changes sign. After spending seven years in Aries, the planet finally moves into your own sun sign of Taurus.

Uranus is the planet of change and the unexpected. It brings upheaval to each house it passes through. For the past few years, you have experienced the effects in your house of inner needs and the unconscious.

Now, and for the next seven years, the winds of change will blow through your house of self. All the energy that has built up within you will now manifest in your conscious life. This can be overwhelming at first. You may experience a strong urge to break free from all your obligations, and embrace a whole new way of life.

This can lead to conflict with people who want you to stay as you are, and you may struggle with doubt and indecision.

Don't be afraid. Although it can be difficult to live through such times, it is necessary. Who wants to be stuck in the same rut forever? Uranus shakes us out of our routines, and gives us the courage to go on new and exciting adventures.

Just be careful not to throw everything overboard. Uranus energy is unpredictable. It can be easy to get carried away, and clear out things that still have great value and worth in our lives. Tread cautiously.

You will have time to think things over after the initial burst of energy, because Uranus will retrograde back into Aries towards the end of the year. This gives you the chance to adjust your plans, reconnect with your own inner self, and reflect on what you want from the future.

Also, since Uranus is a slow-moving planet, there will be plenty of opportunity for adjustment while it travels through your own sun sign. Don't feel that you have to settle anything right now.

Around mid-month, you will notice the effects as Uranus crosses over into Taurus. Take note of any unusual or unexpected events that happen at this time. This will give you a good sense of the direction you're heading in.

Important secrets may come out at this time. Accept that it is better to know the truth.

On Tuesday 15 a new moon in your own sun sign of Taurus signals a fresh beginning. It's a good time to start new projects. Uranus is not involved with this new moon, so you should be safe from its erratic influence.

Bear in mind, though, that you may already feel the effects of the impending Mars retrograde in late June. This means you will not have as much forward energy available as you might. Progress may be slow, especially in the area of travel and learning. Mars is in helpful angle to this new moon, though, so if you want to start something, go ahead.

Jupiter retrograde in your house of relationships and Pluto retrograde in your house of travel and learning also add their input to this new moon. You will have more success implementing or building on existing plans and projects than starting anything brand new. Look back to past experiences, and use them to guide you.

People and opportunities from the past may surface at this time. These are lucky for you right now, so do make good use of them.

5|29|18

On Tuesday 29 a full moon in Sagittarius, your house of shared property, brings something to an end. It is also a good time to finish things up. This is a positive, energising full moon, with Mars in helpful angle and Mercury supporting the Sun. You will get a lot done if you concentrate on existing tasks. Don't start anything new.

There may be some emotional overspill in your conversations at this time. Avoid sensitive topics if you can. It may be best to work alone.

Mars Rules House #1

"inner need + unconciousness

"Self

House #2 =

Career

June 2018

All through the month, you will feel the effects of the impending Mars retrograde. Because Mars is the planet of aggressive energy, this puts the brakes on everything that needs a bit of get-up-and-go. Progress in all areas may be slow, and tempers could rise. Frustration is inevitable.

Try not to get caught up in all the negativity. Use this backward-looking energy to go over past projects, fix any faults, and decide how to move forward in the future.

Mars is currently in Aquarius, your career house, so you will feel the effects most strongly in this area. Since Mars rules your house of inner needs and the unconscious, you may take problems too much to heart. Try not to let them unsettle you.

With Uranus in hard angle in Taurus, your own sun sign and house of self, unexpected snags could crop up in areas that matter to you personally. Be on your guard.

On Wednesday 13 a new moon in Gemini, your money house, signals the start of something. It would usually be a good time to begin new projects, but with Mars slowing down and Neptune in hard angle, it is best to wait. Your ideas may be misguided, and you won't have much positive energy to support you.

Use the time to think about what you want to see happen in this area of your life. Mercury, ruler of Gemini, lends support from Cancer, your house of day-to-day matters. There is a lot of emotion in the air, so don't get too wrapped up in your feelings. Stay calm and think clearly.

On Tuesday 26, Mars turns retrograde in Aquarius, your career house. Expect problems at work during the surrounding days. Everyone will be caught up in this, so try to be patient. Avoid conflict and confrontation if you can. Take great care in safety matters.

Mars will continue retrograde until late August, and the effects will continue throughout September. Everything will seem to be in a holding pattern until then. Stay positive, and don't let frustration get the better of you. Use the time to improve your plans!

On Thursday 28 a full moon in Capricorn, your house of travel and learning, brings something to an end. Saturn retrograde in close support may bring clarity about something or someone from your past. Uranus in helpful angle signals change. Whatever ends now, you are better off without it.

Don't rush into any decisions, though. If you feel the need to put an end to something yourself, wait a while. Emotions may cloud your judgement, and you may be overly pessimistic. The Moon is never happy in Capricorn, and Saturn can be a wet blanket at the best of times. Really think it over. Make sure you're not making a terrible mistake.

July 2018

Throughout the month, Mars continues retrograde in Aquarius, your career house. Uranus, ruler of Aquarius, is in hard angle in Taurus, your own sun sign and house of self. This shows an explosive situation. Your ambitions may be thwarted by career obstacles and hostile forces. Conflict is likely, especially with men. Try to stay calm.

Change is coming, whether you like it or not. If the world seems to be falling apart around you, just let go and have faith that better things are on their way.

Don't start anything new. An eclipse in Aquarius at the end of the month will bring massive upheaval. Nothing will ever be quite the same again. Don't make plans or reach any decisions right now. Let the chips fall, and see how they land.

At mid-month, before the Aquarius eclipse, we have an eclipse in Cancer, your house of day-to-day matters. This is a new moon solar eclipse, and opens a new series of eclipses along the Cancer-Capricorn axis. Over the next two years, ending in July 2020, this series will transform the areas of your life governed by your houses of everyday routines, travel, and learning.

This will expand your horizons and may completely alter the structure of your ordinary routine. Relocation, retraining, and a change of job are all possible. Don't commit to anything

Relocation, retraining
+ Δ Job possible

important until the eclipses have spoken in full. Everything is in flux during these two years, and circumstances may change radically.

The opening eclipse occurs on Friday 13, which may seem fitting. It is intensely emotional, and the effects will be magnified because the Moon is the ruler of Cancer.

Pluto retrograde in opposition in Capricorn suggests someone may try to dominate you, or you may run into practical difficulties that stop you in your tracks.

Jupiter in Scorpio and Neptune retrograde in Pisces form beautiful supporting aspects and will protect you. Stay true to your vision.

A friend or partner may prove helpful. Reach out to people you trust if you feel the need for support.

There is a lot of retrograde energy around right now. You may come up against issues from your past. Recognise that you may be a little fragile at this time, and take good care of yourself.

Take no action unless it's absolutely necessary. Put off any decisions until a less sensitive time. It's fine to respond to events if you must, but don't try to make things happen. Do as little as possible under this eclipse.

Adding to your problems this month, Mercury is turning retrograde in Leo, your house of home and family. You will feel the effects of this from the second week onwards.

Mercury is the planet of thinking and speaking, buying and selling, travel and learning. All of these things will become more difficult as Mercury slows down. Expect computer glitches, misunderstandings, travel snarlups, and all sorts of communication breakdowns.

Problems with your home environment may come to light. Remember that it's better to know these things, so that you can fix them. Don't do anything major, though. Clean up as best you can, and prepare for large-scale renovations at a later date.

Things will be especially fraught in the days surrounding Thursday 26, when the planet changes direction. Tread softly at that time. This is also when we have the next eclipse in the Leo-Aquarius series, so the atmosphere will be electric. Do as little as possible.

Above all, do not make any important decisions. Things are just too frazzled and confusing right now. Respond as best you can to any issues that come up, but don't start anything yourself.

Listen patiently to what the stars are telling you. There will be plenty of time to act later on.

The eclipse takes place on Friday 27, and is a full moon lunar eclipse in Aquarius, your career house. It is the sixth eclipse in the Leo-Aquarius series, affecting your houses of home, family, and career.

31

Each series of eclipses is united by a common theme. If you think back over the changes you have seen in these areas of your life since early 2017, you may get a sense of the way in which this series is transforming your life.

If not, don't worry. Eventually it will become very clear.

Either way, something will end now in the area of your career, and the effects could be cataclysmic.

This is an extremely difficult eclipse, with Mars retrograde near the Moon in Aquarius opposing the Sun in fiery Leo (which it rules), and Uranus in Taurus, your own sun sign and first house of self, in hard angle to both. Prepare for fireworks.

There may be a risk of accidents, injuries, or physical harm. Take great care of your own and other people's safety (especially children).

Beware of aggressive confrontations, as they may turn violent.

Saturn retrograde in Capricorn, your house of travel and learning (which it rules), in helpful angle to Uranus may help put the brakes on and ensure common sense prevails. An older and wiser person may step in to calm an inflamed situation.

If you are mature and experienced, you may need to perform this role. Jupiter in Scorpio and Pluto retrograde in Capricorn are both well aspected, so draw on your understanding and expertise.

Unless you absolutely must, though: Do nothing under this eclipse. Take no risks. Initiate no actions. With so much fiery energy all over the place, there is no telling what will happen. Stay down and wait for everything to blow over.

Mars is still retrograde in your career house, moving into your house of travel and learning at mid-month. As before, this suggests frustration and slow progress, so be patient. Use the time to review past actions rather than start anything new.

With the Sun and Mercury retrograde both in your house of home and family, opposite, this is an excellent time to reconsider your position. Perhaps you've missed some warning flags, or skated over possible problems. Heed them now.

Mars will turn direct at the end of the month, but will not be up to full speed until early October. Don't take any drastic action until then. *No action till Mid Oct*

Also at mid-month, on Saturday 11, we have a new moon and solar eclipse in Leo. This is the seventh eclipse in the Leo-Aquarius series, affecting your houses of home, family, and career.

The series started with a lunar eclipse in Leo, your house of home and family, in mid-February 2017, which brough something to an end.

You now have only one eclipse left in this series, a lunar eclipse in Leo in January next year (2019). That will bring another ending in this same area, and conclude the changes that have occurred in your home and work environments during the past two years. *Jan 2019*

Aug 2018

Right now, though, something new will begin in the area of home and family. This is a positive change, although it may be tough on your feelings. The Sun, the Moon, and Mercury retrograde are all clustered together in Leo (which is ruled by the Sun). This shows positive energy and clear thinking. You may hear news of someone from your past.

Since Mercury rules your house of romance and children, something may come up in this area. Possibly an ex could reappear in your life. Mercury also rules your money house, so there may be unexpected bills.

Jupiter in hard angle in Scorpio, your relationship house, suggests conflict and emotional tension. Either you or someone else may take things a little too seriously. Try to find common ground.

8/19/8

Mercury turns direct in Leo on Sunday 19, so expect a lot of static in the air. Computer glitches, travel snarlups, and misunderstandings of all kinds are likely. You will mostly notice problems in the area of home and family, but be careful when it comes to romance, children, and money issues as well, since Mercury rules these houses. Take special care of children at this time.

Do not sign contracts, make important decisions, or buy anything expensive. The days around Mercury's change of direction are always difficult, and the recent eclipse will make things worse. Keep your head down as much as you can.

8/26/18 — Friendship Ends

On Sunday 26, a full moon in Pisces brings something to an end in the area of friendship. This covers personal friends, but also any groups, clubs, and organisations you belong to.

With realistic Saturn, erratic Uranus, and dreamy Neptune all retrograde at the same time, there is a strong tendency to look backwards. This is a good thing. Allow yourself to make peace with the past, before you move on into the future.

On the following day, Monday 27, energy planet Mars turns direct in Capricorn, your house of travel and learning. Expect a lot of static around this time. Guard against accidents.

Don't rush into action just yet. With all the long-range planets retrograde, there's a lot of slow-moving energy around, and Mars won't be up to full speed until early October. Take your time. Consider carefully what you want to do. Someone from your past, perhaps an older person whom you trust, may give you good advice.

September

9|2018

This month we have two inner planets moving in slow motion. Energy planet Mars is still groggy from the recent retrograde, and won't be up to full speed until early October. Meanwhile, harmony planet Venus, your personal ruler, is slowing down before its impending retrograde around the same time.

This basically means: wait. For you, it may be a time of uncertainty. Perhaps you are unsure of the way forward, or you may be held back by obstacles and lack of support. This can be frustrating, but it is really a blessing in disguise. You have the chance to review the past and learn from experience. Use this time to reflect on what you want or need, and make plans for how to achieve it. *want? Need*

There is one exception: the new moon in Virgo, your house of romance and children, on Sunday 9. This signals a fresh beginning, and is an excellent time to start something new - provided you are returning to existing plans or working with people and projects from your past. If things didn't quite work out for you back in March, this is the perfect opportunity to try again.

Idealistic Neptune retrograde in opposition will draw your mind back to what happened before, while powerful Pluto retrograde in support will provide lots of energy to fix what went wrong. Mercury is now in full forward motion, and in close support in Virgo (which it rules), which will help you see exactly what to do. This time everything will be just right. Go for it! 9/25/18 Full Moon

On Tuesday 25 a full moon in Aries brings something to an end. This is a difficult full moon, tense and emotional. Conflict is likely, perhaps with important people in your life. You may discover something you preferred not to hear.

You will be deeply affected by this full moon, since it takes place in your house of inner needs. Now is a good time to reach clarity about yourself and your life. Perhaps you are on the wrong path, or something you wanted turns out not to be right for you after all. This can be hard to deal with. Take the very best care of yourself.

Do as little as possible under this full moon. Allow feelings to surface, but don't let them take over completely. Try to understand what the real problem is. Then you can work out how to fix it.

October 10/2018

The first week of this month will be frazzled, as Venus turns retrograde on Friday 5. Venus is the planet of love and harmony, so when it reverses direction we tend to get a lot of static in the area of personal relationships.

Since Venus rules your own sun sign, you feel the effects more than most. To make matters worse, the planet is currently in Scorpio, your relationship house. Expect conflict and disagreements within close and established relationships, and difficulties getting along with people in general.

You may also experience health problems, since Venus rules your house of health. Erratic Uranus retrograde in hard angle in Taurus, your own sun sign, brings its own fractious energy into the mix. Old injuries may flare up. Beware of accidents.

With all this angry energy in the air, it is not the best time to move forward on any important projects. Certainly don't start anything new. 10/9/18 = New Moon

On Tuesday 9 a new moon in Libra, your house of health, signals the beginning of something. Pluto in hard angle in your house of travel and learning suggests conflict, perhaps with an authority figure. You may need to assert yourself, but be diplomatic if you can. Avoid aggressive confrontations: just state your case clearly.

Mars is now in full forward motion in Aquarius, your career house, so there is energy available for work projects. Uranus, the ruler of Aquarius, is retrograde in Taurus, your own sun sign, and under stress from retrograde Venus. Progress will be slow, and may ruffle a few feathers.

You may have trouble getting your ideas across, or you may feel pushed around by other people. Still, any plans you made in June can be put into action now.

On Wednesday 24 a full moon in your own sun sign of Taurus brings something important to an end. If you have been working to complete a special project, now is a good time to finish up.

This is a tough full moon, with Uranus and Venus both retrograde, and at odds with each other. Your head may be at war with your heart, or you may crave freedom from your commitments.

Other people's needs and wishes may be crowding out your own. Saturn in helpful angle suggests you need to stay realistic. An older and wiser person may offer support.

November   11/2018

This month you will feel the effects of Venus retrograde in Libra, your house of health. You will experience them more strongly than most other signs, because Venus is your personal ruler and also rules Libra. Illness, injury, and health issues of all kinds are likely. Healing will be slow. Take very good care of yourself.

Venus is the planet of love, and brings harmony to all relationships. In retrograde, this can mean a return to the past. Old flames may come back into your life, or you may rekindle the fire in a relationship that has gone stale.

Conversely, the retrograde can bring snags and problems, especially with people you care deeply about. Progress is difficult. The best you can do is relax and allow everything to happen at its own pace.

Relationships of all kinds will be fraught, but if they are basically strong you should still be fine. Use this time to revisit existing issues and find ways to resolve them. Don't begin any new relationships, whether romantic or otherwise, as they are unlikely to last.

You will also notice the effects of Mercury's impending retrograde in Sagittarius, your house of shared property. Mercury retrograde brings snags and glitches in the areas of thought and speech, agreements and contracts, buying and selling, and travel. Be clear in all your communications, and get everything in writing if you can.

Avoid making expensive purchases or signing contracts. Put off any major decisions until the new year.

Since Mercury rules your money house, be especially careful in matters of finance. It is an excellent time to review existing arrangements, but don't start anything new.

Mercury also rules your house of romance and children, so expect problems in this area. Take especially good care of any children in your life.

Lovers' tiffs and similar disagreements are likely, but don't let them cause you distress. Instead, treat them as a chance to learn more about the people you love.

On Wednesday 7 a new moon in Scorpio, your house of relationships, brings the start of something new. This is a friendly moon, with lovely support from idealistic Neptune in Pisces, your house of friendship, and powerful Pluto in Capricorn, your house of travel and learning.

This is a splendid time to embrace unfamiliar ideas. Expand your horizons!

Neptune retrograde suggests that issues from the past will come up, but in a peaceful way. Take this opportunity to understand more about yourself and the people you care for.

Also on Wednesday 7, Uranus retrogrades back into Aries, your house of inner needs and the unconscious. This may bring unexpected problems. People and events from the past may resurface in surprising ways.

Use this as an opportunity to review any upsets and obstacles that previously got in the way of what you wanted. Uranus brings freedom, so this is a chance to try again - or to finally let go of something that you know deep down isn't working out as you'd hoped.

You have a few months to reflect on these matters and decide what you want to do. Uranus won't leave Aries again until March next year. Then you will be done with upheaval in your inner life, and be ready to move on towards exciting new developments in your outward existence.

Right now there is one more big event to contend with. On Thursday 8, Jupiter moves into Sagittarius, your house of shared property. This is a massive change, and will benefit you for the next year. You may not notice it straight away, but it will become obvious during the coming months.

Jupiter is extra strong in Sagittarius because it rules that sign, so you will feel the planet's blessing in the area of shared property, investments, and inheritance. This is an excellent time to review your financial situation, so get the very best professional advice.

It may seem early to plan for Christmas, but if you intend to travel or have a lot to arrange, get as much as possible done now. You only have a few days of positive energy to help you before things become very tense indeed. Aim to set everything in motion during the days immediately following the new moon, 8-10 November. You don't have to complete it all, but do make a start. After that, do as little as possible until mid-December.

If you plan to travel for Christmas, book a date as close to 22 December as you can. Protective Jupiter will have travel planet Mercury under its wing on that date, bringing luck. Make absolutely sure you get your facts straight and your documents in order. Neptune in hard angle could bring confusion and misunderstandings. Watch out for scams.

The days surrounding Friday 16 will be fraught. Venus changes direction on that day, and Mercury the day after. Both are in hard angle to slow-moving planets in retrograde, so you may find that old problems resurface. Don't try to find solutions just now. The atmosphere is too stormy.

Expect misunderstandings, glitches and snarlups of all kinds. There is tension all over the chart, so tread carefully. You may run across problems in the areas of money, romance, children, health and career. Be realistic, and don't try to fix everything at once. You may need to wait some of it out.

On Friday 23 a full moon in Gemini, your money house, brings something to an end. This is an extremely difficult full moon, with hard angles all over the chart. A cluster of planets in opposition in Sagittarius, your house of shared property, suggests that your hopes may be dashed by the realities of life. Perhaps you may lose money, or run up against major expenditure.

Mars and Neptune in hard angle in dreamy Pisces, your house of friendship, warn against deluding yourself. Someone you trusted may let you down badly.

You may experience deep anger, disappointment, and frustration. Don't allow these feelings to run away with you. Be clear about what you want and need, but don't pick fights unnecessarily.

This is a time to make compromises and find joint solutions to long-standing problems. If you find yourself in an argument with someone, try to see the other person's point of view.

That said, beware of showing too much trust. Be mindful of misleading information, even outright scams. Don't allow yourself to be hoodwinked.

With so much tension in the air, there is a real risk of illness or injury. Take good care of your health, and guard against accidents. If you have children, be especially watchful of their safety at this time.

December

If you enjoy last-minute Christmas shopping, you're in luck this year. The first three weeks of the month will be affected by the Venus and Mercury retrogrades, so are not ideal for getting out and doing things. Venus turned direct in mid-November, but is still a bit groggy and not at its best, while Mercury is still retrograde as the month opens.

With both planets in Scorpio, your house of relationships, expect problems in this area. The good news is, you know what to expect by now and can work around it.

Things will be especially frazzled around Thursday 6, when Mercury turns direct. As always when the planet changes direction, this means a lot of static in the air. Expect computer problems, travel snarlups, equipment failures, and misunderstandings of all kinds.

Don't sign contracts or buy anything expensive, and take special care when travelling.

Even if you've ordered something in advance, this is not the best time to collect it. Wait until mid-month if you can.

On Friday 7, a new moon in Sagittarius signals a fresh beginning in your house of shared property. This is a difficult moon, so will add to the confusion. Mars and Neptune close together in Pisces, your house of friendship, are in hard angle and not helping matters. Pisces is the sign of dreams and wishes, an emotional water sign, and ruled by idealistic Neptune. Mars is an aggressive planet, all get-up-and-go, ruler of fiery Aries. These two energies do not blend well together.

You may find yourself torn between ego and ideals, or between a new desire and existing commitments. Possibly someone may attempt to manipulate you by appealing to your better nature. Beware of deluding yourself, or allowing yourself to be misled. An opportunity that seems too good to be true, probably is.

Fortunately, you do have help. Protective Jupiter, the ruler of Sagittarius, is in close support to the Moon, and realistic Saturn is in helpful angle from its own sign of Capricorn, your house of travel and learning. These are strong and steadying influences, which suggest you will find the right answer if you give yourself time to reflect.

New moons provide fresh energy for ten days after they occur, so there is no need to rush headlong into any decisions. Take the time to really think things over. Again, mid-month would be a good time to act if you do decide to take the plunge.

On Saturday 22 a full moon in Cancer, your house of day-to-day matters, brings something to an end. It is also an excellent time to finish things up. Get all your holiday shopping, travel, and practical arrangements done and dusted during the days surrounding this date.

Saturn in Capricorn, your house of travel and learning, is well aspected and close to the Sun. This will help you deal with everything on your to-do list. Uranus retrograde in Aries, your house of inner needs and the unconscious, is in helpful angle and may supply some last-minute inspiration or other happy surprises.

Keep busy at this time. The Moon is under stress from several more forceful planets, so you may be prone to gloomy thoughts. Don't take these too seriously. The feelings are real, but so is the satisfaction of getting things done. Just work through everything methodically, and your mood will lift.

Christmas itself will be harmonious, with happy aspects all over the chart. Only the Moon is a little out of sorts, so you may feel a bit moody or depressed at times. Don't dwell on these feelings. They will pass.

The New Year period also has happy aspects, so you should be able to enjoy yourself whatever your plans may be.

Don't overindulge, though. On 1 January 2019, energy planet Mars moves into Aries, sign of new beginnings, which it rules. This is a time to dust off all your hopes, plans, and ambitions. With energetic Mars in your corner, there is nothing you can't achieve.

The new year starts with a bang. Make sure you're ready for it!

The Year Ahead: 2019

This will be a year of fresh starts. Mars and Uranus both in Aries, the sign of new beginnings, kick things off in January. There is tons of positive energy around for any major changes you want to make in your life, especially regarding secret hopes or long-held plans.

Everyone will feel this energy, although you will be among the signs that experience it most strongly. There is a widespread urge to break loose from commitments and find new freedom. Existing situations and relationships may fracture under the stress, especially if one partner wants to move on while the other resists.

Don't get completely carried away. Uranus can be erratic, and Mars overly aggressive. Conflict is likely. The key is to make it constructive, rather than destructive.

The best way to handle all this electric energy is to think very carefully about what matters most to you. By all means make changes if you genuinely feel they are necessary, but don't throw out good and valuable parts of your life just because they are old and familiar. We all need some stability!

Conversely, you may be the one who's holding on too tight. If that is the case, try loosening your grip a little. Life will always bring change, so find the excitement in new possibilities, and let all that is outworn drift away.

In March both these planets move into Taurus, your own sun sign and house of self. Uranus has already energised this house during 2017, but now it has Mars for company for a few weeks. You will notice the difference. If last year gave you clues about impending changes, they are likely to happen now. Likewise, if you've had to put plans on ice, now you can start taking action again.

Uranus will continue its overhaul of this house for several more years, so don't get too comfortable. The process will be a fairly slow one. Again, the secret is to embrace change when it comes. Resisting Uranus is pointless: it merely forces energy to build up until an explosion occurs, causing an awful lot of damage.

Simply recognise that nothing ever stays the same, and adopt an attitude of curiosity about the future. Wonderful things are coming your way!

Wisdom planet Saturn will remain in Capricorn, your house of travel and learning, throughout the year, testing this area of your life for weaknesses. Because Saturn rules this sign, the effects will be especially strong. Expect all sorts of problems and flaws to come up.

Try to see this in a positive light. You can only fix problems if you know about them. Saturn will help you gain clarity about your situation and work methodically to make any necessary improvements. By the time the planet moves on at the end of 2020, this area of your life will be as good as you can make it.

In the meantime, you may be in for some upheaval. The Cancer-Capricorn eclipse series continues throughout 2019, and most of the eclipses will be in Capricorn. As always, remember that eclipses cannot be prevented or resisted. They simply occur, bringing startling changes to our lives. All we can do is adapt.

On the plus side, the Cancer-Capricorn series is the only one you will be dealing with. The Leo-Aquarius series ends in January 2019, with a lunar eclipse in Leo. After that, the transformation of your houses of home and career is complete. No major events are due in these areas until 2026.

Protective Jupiter remains in Sagittarius, your house of shared property, where you will feel its blessing throughout the year. This house also covers childhood issues and emotional "baggage" of all kinds, so Jupiter will support you as you deal with them once and for all.

In December Jupiter moves on into Capricorn, your house of travel and learning, where it will spend almost all of 2020. This will be a wonderful help to you in dealing with the testing and upheaval that Saturn and the Cancer-Capricorn eclipse series bring to that house.

Pluto is also in Capricorn and will stay there until 2023, but the deep transformation it brings will be far less disruptive. You may not even notice it until you think back over these years, much later in your life. Still, this powerful planet will make sure you have the strength you need to accomplish everything the universe demands of you. Be bold!

Idealistic Neptune remains in Pisces, sign of dreams and wishes. This is the time to think deeply about what you most want out of life. Saturn in supportive angle will help you work out how to make it come true.

Both these planets are especially strong right now as they are travelling through the signs they rule. This gives a tremendous boost to everything you do, especially in the areas of friendship, travel, and learning. Your horizons will expand. Make the most of it.

This year is a fantastic time to start again, in whatever way is right for you. Listen to what your inner self is saying, be clear about what you truly want out of life, and use the wonderful energy of the stars to make it happen!

***

QUICK GUIDE TO THE HOROSCOPE

A horoscope is a map of the heavens, showing the location of the planets as seen from the Earth. It is divided into twelve sections named after star constellations, known as the signs of the zodiac. The Sun and Moon count as planets, as does Pluto.

The sign in which the Sun was located at the moment of your birth is of huge importance in shaping your fundamental nature and your outlook on life. This is known as your sun sign. Many people who aren't familiar with their full birth horoscope only know their sun sign, so they often refer to it in a shorthand way as their star sign.

In fact, the sun sign only represents one key aspect of your astrological personality: your conscious self. The other eleven signs also represent important areas of lived experience. All twelve zodiac signs taken together, counting from the sun sign, are known as the solar houses.

By knowing which planets will be in a certain house, and in what angle to other planets in other houses, we can predict the influence they are likely to have in various areas of your life.

Without a detailed individual birth horoscope, as well as knowledge of your personal circumstances, it is not possible for anyone else to predict the exact events you will experience. But you are the expert on your own life! Read the forecasts, and consider how they apply to your specific situation. Then plan accordingly, and be amazed at the results.

ABOUT THE AUTHOR

Zoe Buckden has been an astrologer in private practice for almost thirty years. She lives in the north of England with several cats and the occasional hedgehog.

ABOUT BYRNIE PUBLISHING

We are a small independent publisher specialising in genre
fiction and popular nonfiction.

CPSIA information can be obtained
at www.ICGtesting.com
Printed in the USA
LVOW12s1347261217
560826LV00002B/150/P